D0880048

Louisburg Library
Bringing People and Information Together

Boy Puberty
How to Talk about Puberty and Sex with your Tween Boy

Cath Hakanson

Thanks for buying Boy Puberty: How to Talk About
Puberty and Sex With Your Tween Boy.

As a special Thank You, you can download your
FREE parent guide:

30 of the most common questions kids ask about
puberty (and answers that will make you a badass
mom)

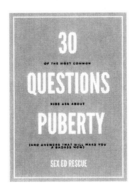

To get it, visit:
https://sexedrescue.com/bp/

ADVANCE PRAISE FOR BOY PUBERTY

"One of the difficulties today is to distinguish who is who on the internet and when it comes to talking about sex, you cannot get someone more prepared, committed, knowledgeable or professional than Cath. I would encourage any parent who wants to talk to their kids about puberty to read and use Cath's work as it provides simple, practical and important information to make the conversation as natural as any other talk parents have with their children."

Dr Madalena Grobbelaar,
Clinical Psychologist,
Psychosexual Therapist & Academic at Women Sexuality Australia

"Cath has created the perfect book for busy parents. Talking about sexuality and relationships can be tricky for most parents – many would rather clean the oven, weed the garden or de-flea the dog, than talk openly and honestly about sex! To this book, Cath has brought her vast experience, wisdom and laugh-a-minute humour."

Dr Lorel Mayberry,
Sexologist and Consultant in Sexuality and Relationship Education,
Department of Sexology, School of Public Health,
Curtin University l President - Borderless Friendship WA Inc

"I find it quite easy to talk to my son about sex, but I still felt a little unsure about puberty. Knowing that there is no 'normal' and that all kids develop in their own way is very reassuring, especially as I noticed my son's first hairs when he was 9. Because of his early signs of puberty, I had already slowly begun to initiate more conversations with him about body changes and sex. But I do know that there are bigger, more involved conversations ahead and so the book is definitely helpful in finding the right words and understanding things from his point of view. I found lots of helpful information and appreciated the conversational style along with the simple 'technical stuff'. So if you have not yet begun to talk to your son, this book will definitely motivate you to start talking as well as help you to feel more comfortable with broaching the subject."

Amanda, Perth, mother of 10 year old boy

"As a mum of a 12 year old boy, this has been an invaluable guide as to what is about to unfold in our household. It explains puberty for boys in a factual but personable way and has given me the knowledge to be able to relate to my son in a crucial time of his life."

Alison, Perth, mother of 2 boys (12 & 6) and 1 girl (11)

"As a father of two boys, I needed this book! It is both concise and comprehensive: Cath doesn't leave anything out but gives us just enough of what we need for every aspect of talking to our kids about puberty. It is a practical step-by-step guide as well as a handy reference, and it even leaves room for a family's cultural and religious beliefs. This is a straightforward yet compassionate handling of a must-have conversation with our kids."

Cory Peppler, teacher, father, and founder of ParentingDigital.com

"The book I wish my mother had read, or at least left lying around! This book has all the finer details to answer the questions I know the basics for. As a mother of 3, and teacher, it's a great resource for age appropriate information."

Ren, mum to 14, 13 and 10 yo question askers

"Cath has such a brilliant way of taking the confusion and awkwardness out of those conversations that can have any of us wondering how to start and what to say. Her simple, no-nonsense wisdom makes this book a must-have for every parent.

The conversations we have with our kids are strengthening and life-giving, but some of the important ones can be a little awkward. Cath offers practical wisdom on how to talk to kids about sex and puberty in ways that will help to relieve the 'awkward' (for them and for you!) and open the communication between you and your child or teen on these essential conversations."

Karen Young, Psychologist, author of *Hey Warrior* and founder of Hey Sigmund

"*Boy Puberty* by Cath Hakanson helps parents of tweens take that first, giant step onto the often bumpy road towards puberty. *Boy Puberty* is a refreshing mix of facts and fun and information for adults looking for the right thing to say and the best way to say it. Puberty can be a roller coaster ride for everyone in the family, and to be armed with the knowledge and skills to negotiate the ride and arrive intact at the other end is exactly what parents and carers need.

Buy the book, read it and study the diagrams before you start to see the body changes and experience the social and emotional whirlwind of puberty. You'll be glad that you did – and so will your son."

Margie Buttriss, HUSHeducation

Boy

PUBERTY

How to Talk about Puberty and Sex

with your

TWEEN BOY

CATH HAKANSON

Boy Puberty: How to Talk About Puberty and Sex With Your Tween Boy by Cath Hakanson

Published by Sex Ed Rescue

PO Box 7903

Cloisters Square WA 6000

Australia

sexedrescue.com

For permission contact:

cath@sexedrescue.com

ISBN-13: 978-0-6481089-5-5

**National Library of Australia
Cataloguing-in-Publication entry(pbk)**

Creator: Hakanson, Cath, author.

Title: Boy puberty : how to talk about puberty and sex with your tween boy / by Cath Hakanson

ISBN: 9780648108955 (paperback)

Subjects: Puberty.

Teenage boys--Health and hygiene.

Teenage boys--Growth.

Table of Contents

Introduction

You're already an expert on puberty because you've been through it yourself.

Maybe you've noticed that your son is starting to smell a bit more like his dad, or that he has hair in some new places. Maybe he isn't showing any signs himself, but you've noticed changes in his friends.

Whichever it is, deep down you realize that it's time to have the talk that you probably never had, or had too late, when you were growing up. It's time to prepare your child for what's to come.

If you're like most parents, including me, preparing your son for puberty probably isn't something you've ever thought about before. And now you realize how unprepared you are to talk about it. Well, you can relax for a moment, because this book will prepare you for what lies ahead. It will tell you everything you need to know before you talk to your son about the changes that will take place in him. This book covers important things, such as what puberty is all about, why it happens, when and how you should start talking, and what you should talk about.

For more than 20 years, I've been helping people get more comfortable with sex. I've answered their questions, listened to their fears, empowered them with the right information, and pointed them

1

in the right direction. After hearing thousands of parents ask me the same questions about puberty over and over again, I've worked out what they want.

Parents want to know how to have honest conversations that will guide their child through puberty and strengthen their relationship without them feeling embarrassed, awkward or nervous.

But they don't know how to start.

This book will help you get started with talking. It will help you to:

- Understand what puberty means for your son, so you are fully prepared to answer his questions.

- Realize the importance of discussing puberty before it starts, so your son isn't surprised, confused or frightened.

- Know the evolving changes that happen during puberty, and when they are likely to happen, so you can confidently identify them and prepare your son for what comes next.

- Create crucial talking points you can use with your son before he gets misinformation from somewhere else, so you have the right information to share at the right time.

- Develop basic tools to help you easily talk to your son, even if he is reluctant to talk about puberty.

This book won't just show you how to talk to your son about puberty. It will show you how to have the type of relationship where he can talk to you about anything, no matter what. But you need to start talking sooner rather than later, because puberty is on its way, whether you like it or not!

As much as we would all like to leave it for someone else to address (me included), you love your son and know that he deserves to hear about the changes that are going to happen to him from you, so that he can turn to you for support, guidance and information.

Empower your son with the right information so that when the time comes, he doesn't make the wrong decisions around love, sex and relationships.

Happy Talking!

What Is Puberty?

Puberty is going to happen whether you want it to or not, but at least it happens gradually.

Puberty can mean many different things, but, basically, it is when your son's body changes from being a child to an adult. It is the last time his body will grow. Puberty isn't the last time that his body will change, though, because, as we know, our bodies will keep on changing for our whole lives. Luckily, puberty doesn't happen overnight. It can take from two-to-five years, up to 10 years for your son's body to change. This is a good thing, as it gives him time to get used to the changes that will slowly be happening to him. Puberty is about more than just his body changing. His relationships with his family, friends and peers will change. His feelings and even his personality will change too.

What does this all mean?

Puberty means your son will soon be fertile, that he can help to make a baby. And that you could become a grandparent! But does this mean that he is ready to become a parent? Most likely not. Just because his body is capable of reproducing doesn't mean he's necessarily ready to become a parent, but he does need to know that this could happen.

When will puberty happen?

The time puberty starts is different for everyone. It can be earlier for some boys and later for others. Everyone is different. Usually, puberty will start sometime between the ages of nine and 15. When your son's body is the right size and shape for him, the hormones that start the changes will be triggered, and his body will begin to change. It is important to remember that you can't rush or delay puberty. This can be hard for some boys, especially if they haven't had their growth spurt, and are the shortest boy in their class. They will see themselves as being different from their friends, and will wonder if they are normal.

If he's an early bloomer, your son may be teased about being smelly or having man-boobs. He will most likely be wondering what's wrong with him, as he is the only one whose body is changing. If he's a late bloomer, he may be worried that he hasn't yet started to change, and he will wonder what is wrong with him. It is important that your son understands that puberty will happen when his body is ready for it, and that everybody is different.

If you started puberty early, the chances are that your son will be an early bloomer. If you started puberty late, your son may be a late bloomer too.

When to worry

Some boys start puberty earlier or later than you would expect. An early start to puberty is called precocious puberty. It is a lot more common in girls than it is in boys. Precocious puberty in boys is when before the age of nine, they show signs of:

- Growth of the testicles and penis.
- Growth of pubic, underarm or facial hair.

- Rapid height growth, i.e. a growth spurt.
- Voice deepening.
- Acne.
- Adult body odor.

If any of this happens to your son before the age of nine, you should seek medical advice. If your son does not have any physical signs of puberty by the age of 14, you should seek medical advice regarding why puberty is delayed. For most boys, puberty may be late because it was also late in one or both parents. It could also be delayed because of a hormonal imbalance, being underweight, or being under extreme stress. Rarely, developmental or chromosomal abnormalities can be found.

What makes puberty happen?

Hormones are responsible for making the changes to your son's body during puberty. Hormones are chemicals that all our bodies make. They travel throughout the body in our bloodstream, from the place they are made to the place they do their work. Their job is to start something working. During puberty, the job of some hormones is to make the body capable of reproducing.

The pituitary gland

During puberty, it all starts because of a gland at the base of the brain known as the pituitary gland. One day, when the body is ready, the brain sends a message to the pituitary gland that tells it to start releasing growth hormones into the bloodstream. The hypothalamus produces a hormone called gonadotrophin-releasing hormone (GnRH). This hormone stimulates the pituitary gland to release two hormones: follicle-stimulating hormone (FSH) and luteinizing hormone (LH). These hormones travel through the blood to the testicles (testes) to make the hormone testosterone and to get ready to make sperm.

The pituitary gland is the master gland that tells all other glands what to do. It tells the other glands to start making the hormones that are needed to turn your child into an adult. Hormones are the chemical messages that allow different parts of the body to communicate with each other. Think of it like a telephone line, where everyone's telephones are connected by wire cables, and we can send messages (talk) through the telephone lines. The body has its own telephone lines (bloodstream), where the glands are sending hormones (chemical messages) to the different parts of the body.

Follicle-stimulating hormone

Follicle-stimulating hormone (FSH) has an important job to do. When FSH reaches the testicles, it spurs the growth of the seminiferous tubules, which is where sperm is made. Over a couple of years, the testicles will slowly grow bigger, as all this new growth happens inside of them.

During puberty, the testicles will grow to about the size of a plum.

This can take a couple of years to happen. Once these tubules are fully grown, the body is then ready to start maturing the sperm to be ready for reproduction. In boys, this means that they will now be able to ejaculate, and semen, which contains the sperm, will come out of their penis.

THE PITUITARY GLAND

The pituitary gland sends a message to the testicles, telling them to start making testosterone and sperm.

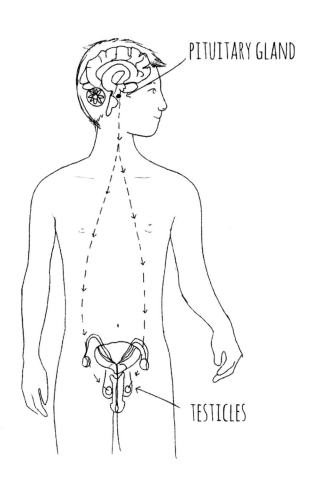

PITUITARY GLAND

TESTICLES

SEMINIFEROUS TUBULES

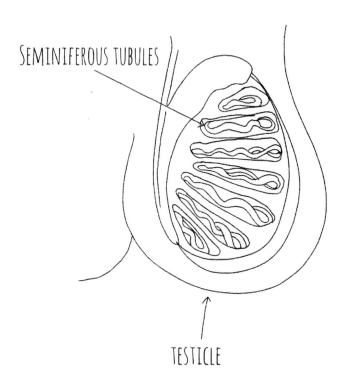

SEMINIFEROUS TUBULES

TESTICLE

Luteinizing hormone

Luteinizing hormone (LH) has a different job to do. It triggers special cells inside the testes, called Leydig cells, to start producing hormones called androgens. The main androgen that the Leydig cells make is called testosterone. Girls have testosterone too, but not as much as boys. Androgens are hormones that tell the body that it's time to mature or grow up. It helps to make the male changes that boys have, things like a deeper voice, face/armpit/pubic hair, and the start of their sex drive.

Testosterone helps to get certain parts of the body, like the prostate gland and the seminal vesicles, ready to care for and carry the mature sperm. When everything is ready, testosterone will then tell the testicles that it is time to start maturing the sperm to be ready for reproduction via ejaculation. In boys, this means that they will now be able to ejaculate, and semen, which contains the sperm, will come out of their penis.

Sperm

Sperm or spermatozoa are the male reproductive cells. Sperm are a bit different to the
reproductive cells that girls have. Girls are born
with their ova or eggs, whereas boys aren't born
with their sperm. During puberty, the testicles
will start to make sperm for the very first time.
When all the reproductive organs are fully grown,
you son's body will be capable of ejaculating. This
means he is now fertile and will eventually be
capable of creating a baby, if his sperm joins with
an egg during sexual intercourse.

Technically speaking, though, your son
won't be capable of producing enough sperm to
fertilize an egg through sexual intercourse until
after about six-to-18 months of ejaculating. But,
to keep things simple, it is best to think of him
as being fertile once he begins to ejaculate. You
don't want to become a grandparent too soon!

Sperm are so tiny they can't be seen without a microscope.

Erection

An erection is when the penis becomes stiff and hard, larger and longer, and stands out from the body. Erections happen to boys all the time – from when they are a fetus growing inside their mother's uterus, and right through their childhood.

As boys go through puberty, erections begin to happen more frequently and for a different reason. Now they start to happen so that the sperm can get to the ovum (egg) and fertilize it. For this to be happen, the penis needs to be erect, so that it can be pushed into the vagina, where the sperm is delivered, and fertilization can happen.

ERECTION

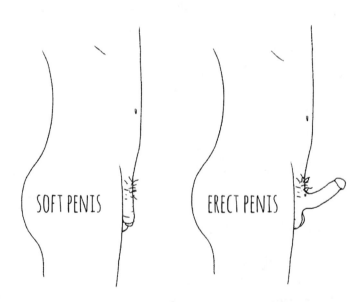

SOFT PENIS   ERECT PENIS

Erections are all about an increased blood flow to the penis. The brain sends a chemical message to the blood vessels in the penis. The arteries relax and open to let more blood in. At the same time, the veins close, trapping the blood inside the penis. There is a lot of spongy tissue inside the penis. When it is filled with blood, that soft spongy tissue will go firm or hard, making the penis expand, because of all the extra blood inside it. The penis will become larger, firmer, and stand out from the body. It is now erect. When the erection is over, the veins will relax, letting the extra blood back into the body. At the same time, the arteries will close, only letting a small amount of blood into the penis. The penis then becomes soft again.

Ejaculation

Ejaculation is when sperm are suddenly released from the body. This can only happen when the penis is erect. It can happen during sex, masturbation, or during a "wet dream" (also called nocturnal emission).

When the body is getting close to ejaculation, the sperm will begin their journey to leave the body. Sperm are made in the testicles. They then mature in coiled tubes attached to the top of each testicle – the epididymis. When the body is getting close to ejaculation, the mature sperm travel up into the body through some tubes called the vas deferens. On their way, they mix with different fluids from the seminal vesicles and the prostate gland. This mixture of sperm and fluid is now called semen. Its job is to nourish the sperm and to keep it healthy.

Semen is a creamy white fluid. It can contain millions of sperm, with up to 300-to-500 million sperm coming out at a time!

The semen then travels through a tube that runs down the center of the penis (urethra) and spurts out of the opening at the tip of the penis. Strong muscle contractions squeeze the semen out. An orgasm usually happens with ejaculation, but not always. Sometimes you can ejaculate without an orgasm. It is not easy to explain how an orgasm feels, because it can be different each time. You could describe it as a really nice feeling that starts in the genitals, and can also be felt throughout the whole body. This feeling then begins to feel stronger and stronger, building up until you begin to feel waves of intense feelings. For males, these feelings usually reach their peak with ejaculation, when the sperm comes out of the man's penis, but not always. Sometimes you won't ejaculate with an orgasm. After ejaculation, the penis will become soft and slowly return to its normal size.

EJACULATION

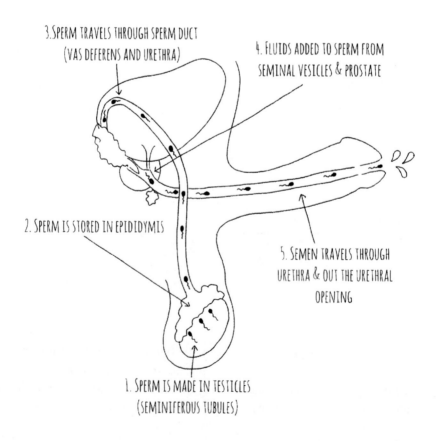

3. SPERM TRAVELS THROUGH SPERM DUCT (VAS DEFERENS AND URETHRA)

4. FLUIDS ADDED TO SPERM FROM SEMINAL VESICLES & PROSTATE

2. SPERM IS STORED IN EPIDIDYMIS

5. SEMEN TRAVELS THROUGH URETHRA & OUT THE URETHRAL OPENING

1. SPERM IS MADE IN TESTICLES (SEMINIFEROUS TUBULES)

Fertilization

This is what happens when the sperm meets the egg. Fertilization usually happens during sexual intercourse, but it can also happen with assistance, for example, with in vitro fertilization (IVF). During sexual intercourse, sperm is released into the vagina when the male ejaculates semen. The sperm will then swim through the vagina and uterus, and up into the fallopian tubes, looking for an egg to fertilize. The egg is fertilized while it is still within the fallopian tube. It will continue travelling along the fallopian tube and into the uterus, where it will attach itself to the thickened uterine lining.

FERTILIZATION

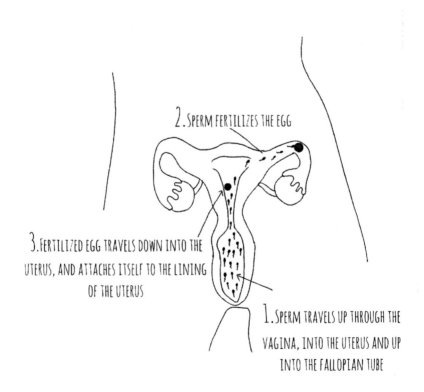

2. SPERM FERTILIZES THE EGG

3. FERTILIZED EGG TRAVELS DOWN INTO THE UTERUS, AND ATTACHES ITSELF TO THE LINING OF THE UTERUS

1. SPERM TRAVELS UP THROUGH THE VAGINA, INTO THE UTERUS AND UP INTO THE FALLOPIAN TUBE

The body parts

When you start talking about puberty, it is important to know the names of the different parts you will be talking about. Below you will find some images and child-friendly definitions your son will understand.

Anus: The opening that is behind the scrotum, where feces (poo) comes out. Girls have an anus too.

Bladder: A stretchy bag that holds the urine (pee) before it comes out of the body. The urine leaves the bladder through a small tube called the urethra.

Corona: The ridge that runs around the bottom of the glans, where it joins the body of the penis.

Cowper's gland: These two small, round glands (the size of a pea) are found underneath the prostate gland. When a man starts to feel sexually aroused, they will start to make a special fluid that will lubricate the penis and keep the sperm safe as it travels through the urethra. The other name for this part is the bulbourethral gland.

Epididymis: The testicle is connected to the epididymis. Once sperm has been made in the testicles, it is sent to the epididymis. It is here that the sperm is grown up or matured, ready for reproduction. If felt through the scrotum, it will feel soft and squishy, like a piece of cooked spiral pasta.

Foreskin: The loose skin at the end of the penis. It protects the end of the penis, the glans, which is very sensitive to touch.

Glans: The head or the tip of the penis. It has many nerve endings, which means it is sensitive to touch. It is usually covered by the foreskin.

Penis: The part that hangs in front of the scrotum and sticks out. Urine (pee) comes out of the small opening at the end of it. The penis is also used for sexual intercourse, where it becomes erect, and semen comes out of the end of it, through the urethral opening.

Prostate gland: A gland that is at the base of the penis near the bladder. The urethra runs through the center of it. The prostate gland helps with bladder control and secretes fluids that mix with the sperm to make semen.

Scrotum: The soft bag of squishy skin between the legs that holds and protects the testicles. It has a muscle which makes it expand with heat (e.g. when having a warm bath) and shrink with cold (e.g. when swimming in the ocean). This keeps the testicles at the right temperature to protect the sperm.

Seminal vesicles: A pair of glands that lie on either side of the bladder. They open into the vas deferens and secrete fluids that mix with the sperm to make semen.

Shaft: The length or body of the penis.

Testicles: The male sex organs that make sperm. They are two soft oval-shaped parts that will grow much bigger during puberty, to about the size of a plum. Sperm is made in the testicles. If felt through the scrotum, a testicle will feel like a hard-boiled egg that has been peeled.

Urethra: A narrow tube that leaves from the bladder, and goes through the penis to the small opening at the tip of the penis (urethral opening). It also carries the semen after it leaves the vas deferens.

Urethral opening: The slit at the end of the penis (through the glans) where urine and semen come out. Girls have a urethral opening too.

Vas deferens: The tube that connects the testicles/epididymis to the prostate and seminal vesicles. If felt through the scrotum, it will feel like a piece of cooked spaghetti.

THE INSIDE PARTS

FRONT VIEW

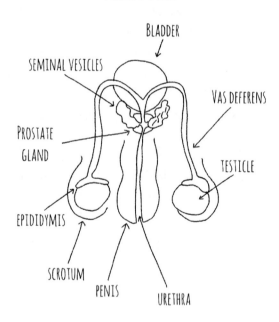

THE INSIDE PARTS

SIDE VIEW

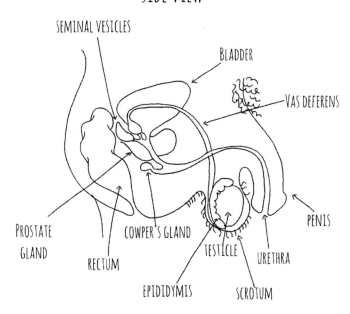

SEMINAL VESICLES

BLADDER

VAS DEFERENS

PROSTATE
GLAND

COWPER'S GLAND

PENIS

RECTUM

TESTICLE

URETHRA

EPIDIDYMIS

SCROTUM

THE OUTSIDE PARTS

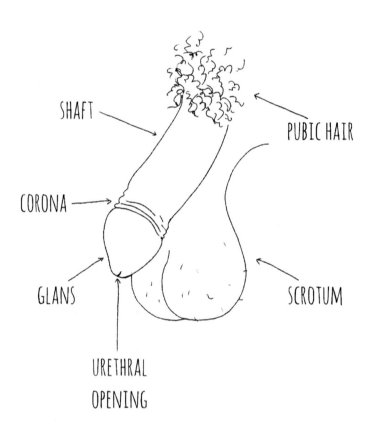

What do kids need to know?

Every boy is different. Some boys will want to know every detail, whereas others will be happy with just the basics. The good thing is you won't be expected to remember all of this, or have to talk about it all. That is where books become invaluable. Books will include all the technical details, which means you don't need to remember everything. A basic understanding will help with answering their questions.

So, what are the main messages we need to give to boys?

- Puberty means your body will change from being a kid to an adult.
- Changes are both physical and emotional.
- Puberty happens to all kids, and it is normal.
- Puberty means you can reproduce.
- Changes are very gradual.
- Puberty happens to girls too, but girls start about two years earlier.
- Puberty doesn't happen overnight; it takes two-to-five years from start to finish. This gives you time to get used to the new you.
- Some kids start sooner, some start later.
- Some kids change quickly, some kids change more slowly.
- Everyone is different.
- Your body is already programmed to create the body that you are meant to have.

Why You Must Talk About Puberty

Don't waste this opportunity to be your child's number-one source for information on love, sex and relationships.

Reasons for talking to boys about puberty

Sometimes it can feel as if there are more reasons not to talk than there are to talk. Will you say too much and overwhelm him? Will you say too little and misinform him? Do boys need to understand puberty differently than girls? How do you approach the topic without embarrassing him or yourself? What if your son shows no interest or covers his ears while walking away?

You're not alone if you have already asked yourself some of these questions, as they are questions that parents commonly ask. If you have some lingering doubts about whether you're doing the right thing, you should know that most parents feel the same. Talking to your son about puberty is one of the greatest gifts you can give him, and yourself.

Here are some of the reasons why you should be talking to him about puberty sooner rather than later:

Puberty will be much easier for him

Boys who know what to expect during puberty will usually have a much better experience than boys who are unprepared. Think back for a moment to your own memories of puberty. Did your parents talk to you about puberty and tell you what to expect? If they did, you are one of the lucky few! Most of us don't have very good memories of our own journey through puberty. We didn't have parents who spoke to us about puberty. Or if we did, it was usually the one big talk that we didn't really understand, which meant that we had to go through puberty unprepared for what was going to happen to us. So, we know that boys will cope much better with puberty when they know what to expect. They need to know about what changes are going to happen to them, why it is happening, and how to take care of their new body. You aren't alone if you want your son to have a much better experience of puberty than the one you had.

He'll hear about puberty anyway

Unless you live in the middle of nowhere with no contact with the outside world, your son will eventually hear about puberty. He will hear his friends talk about it at school, as they whisper about growing hair down there, or about how big their penis is, or as they giggle and point out the girls with their newly-developing breasts. He will hear about it in class. Reproduction, and the changes that happen to our bodies, is in most school curriculums around the world. Don't be surprised if one day he brings a letter home from school advising you about these forthcoming lessons. He may learn about puberty from his favorite TV show, on the internet, or in a book.

Regardless of whether you have talked about puberty or not, your son is eventually going to hear about it. The problem is that what he hears will often be negative and inaccurate. This means that it is really important for you, the parent, to be the one who tells him all about puberty. This is your opportunity to provide him with the right information in a way that prepares him instead of scaring him. More importantly, puberty is a great time to start talking to your son about what sexual behaviors and attitudes are okay, and not okay, in your family. Your son is now reaching the age where he will start forming his own attitudes and beliefs about sexuality. By sharing yours with him, you are providing him with a moral compass to guide him as he makes sense of the mixed messages that he receives from the media, his peers, and the world around him.

Kids want us to talk to them about growing up

Research tells us that 12-to-15-year-olds consistently say their parents are the most important influence when it comes to making decisions about sex, even more than their friends, the media, religious leaders, their brothers or sisters, or their teachers. Parental influence does decline as kids get older, though, which means that it is important to start talking sooner rather than later.[1]

Kids are now shaping their lifelong values

This is the time your son will be working out his own thoughts, beliefs and attitudes about the world around him. He will be making important decisions about what attitudes and behaviors are okay, and not okay, when it comes to love, sex and relationships. Which is why it is so important that you are there to guide him. You can't tell your son what his values and beliefs will be, you can only guide him. Do you have the exact same values as your parents? Probably not. You may share some of the same values as your parents, but you will also have some that are yours alone. And your siblings will have a completely different set of values too, despite the fact that you were all influenced by your parents in the same way. The reason that you share some of the same values as your parents is because they influenced you. Some of their values must have made sense, and you took them on board as your own. And some you developed by yourself, influenced by what you saw on TV, heard in music, or learned by talking with your friends and by watching your peers.

Your son will be the same. He will make up his own set of values but he will listen to what you say. If you don't share your values with your son, you can't expect to have any influence on what sexual

---

1 The National Campaign to Prevent Teen and Unplanned Pregnancy. (2016). Survey Says: Parent Power Washington, DC: Author.

attitudes and behaviors he develops. If you want to have any say in it, you will have to talk to him, and explain why you feel the way you do.

A stronger relationship

By having open and honest conversations about it, you can guide your son through puberty and strengthen your relationship. As much as you'd like to leave it up to someone such as the school or his friends to address the issue, you love your son and know he deserves to hear from you about the changes happening to him. This way, he'll be confident about what comes next, knowing that he can turn to you for support, guidance and information.

Research tells us that it is easier for teens to delay sexual activity and to avoid teen pregnancy when they are able to have open, honest conversations about these topics with their parents. Overall closeness between parent and child, shared activities, parental presence in the home, and parental caring and concern, were all associated with a reduced risk of early sex and teen pregnancy. Teens who are close to their parents and feel supported by them are more likely to delay sex, to have fewer sexual partners, and to use contraception.[2]

You already know a lot about puberty

You have firsthand experience of puberty. You have already been through it and know what it can be like. You know what it is like to find that first hair, the embarrassment of being teased for having breasts, or feeling embarrassed as someone you really like walks past and looks at you. Sharing stories from your own journey through puberty helps your son know that you have been there, and that you understand what he is going through.

A more confident child

Boys who know what to expect from puberty are going to be a lot more accepting of the changes they will soon be experiencing. They will feel a lot more positive about their bodies and feel good

---

2 Albert, B. (2012). With One Voice 2012: America's Adults and Teens Sound Off About Teen Pregnancy. Washington, DC: The National Campaign to Prevent Teen and Unplanned Pregnancy.

about being a boy. They will also be a lot more accepting of their own individual differences, and be happy with who they are instead of unhappy about who they aren't![3] It is helpful for boys to know that what is happening to them is normal, and that it is happening to their friends too.

Good practice for even trickier conversations

The more you talk about tough topics like puberty, the easier it gets. Eventually, you will be able to talk to your son without feeling as embarrassed, awkward or nervous. By the time you get around to some of the other tough topics, such as dating and sex, you'll have had a bit of experience, and you will find it a lot easier than if you were starting afresh. There are plenty of good reasons why you should be talking to your son about puberty sooner rather than later.

---

3 Goldman, R & Goldman, J. (1988). Show me yours! Understanding children's sexuality. Ringwood. Penguin Books.

When To Start Talking About Puberty

Puberty will start when your body is ready for it. You can't rush it, stop it or make it slow down!

When is a good time to start talking?

There are a few signs that you can look out for that will let you know.

You should be ready to start talking to your son about puberty if:

1. He is starting to grow pubic and/or underarm hair.
2. He has pimples or a strong body odor.
3. He has had a sudden growth spurt and has outgrown his shoes very quickly.
4. You notice that his friends are suddenly a lot taller, that they smell and/or have pimples.
5. He is between nine-and-14 years old.
6. He starts to ask you questions about puberty.

What age should I expect to see changes?

You'll start to see physical changes in your son anywhere between the ages of 10 and 14, but usually between 12 and 13. Remember, every boy is different. Some boys will be earlier or later than their friends. Some may have their changes in a slightly different order. Every boy is different, and it is usually normal.

When is it too early to talk?

You can start talking to kids about puberty from a very young age. By talking when they are younger, you are gently introducing the concept to them that one day their body will start to change from being a child's body to an adult body. Kids as young as three or four will have no trouble grasping this concept. They won't really understand why, or even want to know, but they will accept it as just another thing that will one day happen to them. They will see puberty as being normal.

There are many possible opportunities for talking about puberty to young children. Your three-year-old might walk into the bathroom when you're changing your tampon or pad. He might ask why you're bleeding down there. Your five-year-old might have noticed that his father has pubic hair and wants to know when he too will get hair down there. Your seven-year-old might be upset because his 13-year-old sister won't have a bath with him anymore, and he wants to know why. These are all situations where you can provide your son with basic information that will satisfy his curiosity. You don't need to worry about giving him too much information. Anything he doesn't understand, will be forgotten because it just doesn't make sense to him.

When is it too late to talk?

Sometimes you can wait too long to start talking about puberty, especially if your son has already started to have wet dreams. If this is your situation, it still isn't too late. It is better to be late than to never talk at all. You still have the opportunity to be able to prepare your son for what comes next and to let him know that he can turn to you for support, guidance and information.

Can Moms talk to sons about puberty?

There is no reason why mothers can't talk to their sons about puberty. Some boys are comfortable talking about their changing body with their mother, and some boys aren't. Let your son be the guide regarding what he is comfortable with. If you get the sense that he isn't comfortable, try to involve a man that he trusts, such as an uncle, an older cousin, or a family friend.

Whether moms join in the conversations or not, just being there for your son is enough. Just acknowledging that his body is changing, or letting him know that you are there for him, is enough. By letting your son know that puberty is all okay, that you know what happens, that you are proud of him, and love him, is incredibly helpful.

What Changes Happen During Puberty?

We all have the same changes. For some, they happen in a different order, sooner or later, faster or slower. But at the end of the day, he'll have a grown-up body.

A time of change

Puberty is that time when your son will change from a child to an adult. Luckily these changes happen slowly over a two-to-10-year period, which means that your son has plenty of time to get used to his new body. The first changes that happen with puberty are hidden, as they happen on the inside. From around the age of nine or 10, your son's body will slowly start to release hormones. It isn't until he is around 12-to-13 years old that you will start to see any changes to the outside of his body. For some boys, they can be as young as 9 or as old as 13 to 14. The important thing to remember is that each boy will grow at his own pace, which is the pace that is right for his body.

Changes to his body

There are many visible and invisible changes that will happen during this time. Some of the changes that happen to your son's body will be easy to spot, but others won't be, as they are hidden inside his body. Although the timing of puberty can be different for every boy, the sequence of changes that will happen to your son is more predictable.

Below you will find a rough guide to the changes you can expect and when. Not every boy will follow this pattern, but it will give you an idea of what to expect. Many of the changes during puberty will also overlap each other, and may happen over several years. Remember, every boy is different and almost anything can be normal. If concerned, talk to your family doctor.

Nine to 12 years

Hidden changes

The first changes that will happen to your son are hidden, as they are happening deep inside his body. The body will start to release hormones that will trigger changes to start happening. The main hormone for boys is testosterone. It will begin to surge in your son's body, causing his testicles to grow and make sperm. No changes can yet be seen outside his body, other than some growth of the scrotum and testicles. Some boys may have a growth spurt, and some may start to grow very fine hairs in the pubic area.

Nine to 15 years
(Average 11 to 13 years)

Testicles

Your son's testicles will continue to slowly grow, with one testicle now beginning to hang lower than the other. This prevents the testicles from knocking each other. His scrotum will also hang lower, becoming darker in color, thinner and less smooth. If your son has pale skin, his scrotum will become more reddish in color, while with dark skin, it will deepen in color.

Penis

Your son's penis will remain unchanged. It may grow slightly larger, but usually there is little or no change at all. He may start to have erections more frequently, but he still isn't ejaculating.

Hair growth

Fine hair may begin to grow at the base of the penis and scrotum. These first hairs are usually long, slightly pigmented (colored) and straight or slightly curly. It is normal for some boys not to grow hair just yet.

Growth spurt

Your son will start to grow taller and the shape of his body will begin to change. Before he grows taller, his feet and hands will usually have a growth spurt of their own. Your son will also gain weight as he starts to develop muscle, and as his bones grow bigger.

If you find yourself joking about him going up a shoe size overnight, then you can be certain that puberty is on its way!

Body odor

It is during puberty that your son will start to sweat. This means that his body odor will change, especially when it comes from his armpits.

Breasts

The skin around the nipples, known as the areola, will darken and start to increase in size.

11 to 16 years
(Average 13 ½ to 15 ½ years)

Testicles

Your son's testicles and scrotum will continue to grow. Sperm production may begin for some, but not all, boys, i.e. ejaculation. Boys usually discover this during masturbation, or they might wake up in the morning with wet pants after a wet dream (nocturnal emission).

Penis

Your son's penis will start to grow. It will grow longer, rather than wider. Erections will be a lot more common than before, often at the wrong time, or in the wrong place.

Hair growth

Some boys may only now be starting to develop pubic hair. It will become darker, thicker and curlier, and start to cover a much wider area. Hair will continue to grow on his legs and underarms.

Growth spurt

Your son's body will still be growing, and gaining weight and height. Muscles become larger and shoulders broader. He will grow taller and you'll notice that he is a lot hungrier and eating more food as his body tries to keep up with the energy it needs to grow. His face will also begin to change, making him look more mature.

Body odor and skin

Sweat and oil glands will become more active, which can result in acne. Body odor is here to stay.

Voice

His voice will begin to crack as the voice box gets larger.

Breasts

It can be common for boys to experience short-term swelling and tenderness around the nipples. As their shoulders grow wider, this breast tissue will flatten, usually disappearing within one or two years.

11 to 17 years
(Average 15 to 17 years)

Testicles

Your son's testicles and scrotum will continue to grow. The scrotum skin will continue to darken. Boys will now begin to produce sperm, which means that wet dreams (nocturnal emissions) may start to happen, and they will ejaculate with masturbation and sexual arousal. Not all boys will have wet dreams (either is normal).

Penis

His penis will become thicker and longer. The glans, at the end of the penis, will grow wider and develop a distinct edge or corona.

Hair growth

Pubic hair continues to grow, with hair now starting to grow around the anus, and possibly even in a line from the groin up to the navel. Hair will continue to grow on his legs and underarms. Facial hair will start to grow on his face, usually on the upper lip, chin and near the ears.

Growth spurt

Your son will keep on gaining weight and growing taller.

Body odor and skin

We have oil glands all over our bodies, but during puberty, they become a lot more active. Your son's skin may become oily, especially around the chin, nose, forehead, chest and/or back. Some boys may develop acne or pimples. His hair is also more likely to become oily, meaning that he will now need to wash it more frequently.

Voice

His voice will continue to crack at times and deepen.

14 to 18 years
(Average age 17 years)

This is the last stage of changes. Your son will now reach his full height and will look like a young adult. His pubic hair will now cover his groin, and possibly even his inner thighs. His genitals will now be fully grown and will look the same as those of an adult man. Your son will now need to shave, as his facial hair continues to grow. Some boys will begin to grow chest hair.

Changes to his feelings and relationships

Puberty is not just about getting your son's body ready to make babies. It is also about making sure that he is ready to face all the responsibilities that come with being an adult.

While your son's body is changing, his brain will be changing too. He will experience changes in:

- The way he feels about himself.
- His relationship with his parents.
- His friendships and feelings of love.
- What others expect of him.

This is also the time that he will be working out his own thoughts, beliefs and attitudes about the world around him. He will be making important decisions about what attitudes and behaviors are okay, and not okay, when it comes to love, sex and relationships. It is important that you are there to provide your son with the support, guidance and information he needs.

Boys who are prepared for puberty are more likely to find it a breeze instead of a hurricane!

Common feelings

Puberty is not necessarily the nightmare that we are all led to believe it is. Every boy is different regarding how he responds to this time in his life. The one thing we do know is that boys who know what to expect from puberty have a much easier time as they go through it. If your son has a much easier time, it means that you will too.

Common feelings that your son may experience include:

- Struggling with a sense of identity and questions about himself.
- Moodiness, anger and depression.
- Sleeping a bit more than usual.
- Feeling clumsy as he adjusts to bigger feet, longer limbs and increased strength.
- A need for more independence and privacy.
- Relationships with his friends and the opinions of others becoming more important than family.
- Being more concerned or worried about how he looks, with a focus on clothes and his body.
- Worrying about what the future holds (school, family, job, etc.).

- Having crushes on actors, singers, teachers, peers, other kids.
- Being curious about changes that are happening to his body, especially his genitals.
- Feeling sexually attracted to people.
- Being more interested in sex than ever before and perhaps fantasizing and masturbating.
- Masturbation taking on a new meaning due to orgasm and sexual feelings.

As you can see, there is a lot happening. What's important is that your son understands this is all normal and it happens to everyone. His friends will be going through the same things too. It is normal for boys to feel anxious about growing up, and to sometimes wonder if they are going crazy. Think back to your own memories of puberty, and you will know what I mean. Puberty is a time of great change and the more support your son has, the easier a time it will be for him and ultimately for you too.

Puberty for girls

Girls go through puberty too. Some of their changes are the same, and some of them are very different. Girls usually start puberty about two years sooner than boys do.

It is important for boys to know that girls go through puberty too, but about two years earlier, and that some of their changes are the same.

During puberty, changes for girls include:

- Growth spurts.
- Pimples or acne.
- Voice deepens but not as much as it does for boys.

- Oilier hair.
- Hair on arms and legs gets thicker.
- Pubic and underarm hair grow.
- Body odor.
- Hands and feet grow bigger and longer.
- Breasts begin to develop and grow.
- Hips become wider and thighs and bottoms more rounded.
- Uterus and vagina grow and begin to release eggs.
- Periods start (menstruation).
- Mood changes.

Chapter References

Adolescence and Puberty. Edited by John Bancroft and June Machover Reinisch. 1990. Oxford University Press. New York.

Gender Differences at Puberty. Edited by Chris Haywood. 2003. Cambridge University Press. Cambridge.

Handbook of Child and Adolescent Sexuality: Developmental and Forensic Psychology. Edited by Daniel S. Bromberg and William T. O'Donohue. 2013. Elsevier. Academic Press. Oxford.

Puberty: Physiology and Abnormalities by Philip Kumanov and Ashok Agarwal. 2016. Springer International Publishing. Switzerland.

What To Talk To Your Son About

This is all normal and his friends are going through it too. Soon he will be used to his new body and know how to care for it.

A new self-care regime

Puberty is all about change, and your son will soon have a new body to care for. He will need a little bit of advice on how to care for it. Remember, all of this is new to him. What you and I think of as common-sense, such as washing hair more regularly, so it doesn't smell and get oily, isn't as obvious to your son. He needs you to slowly start teaching him a whole new regime of self-care, and he will need a fair bit of reminding before he automatically starts to include these new habits into his everyday life.

What to talk about

Relax, you don't need to talk to your son about every single thing that is listed below. Let your son guide you regarding what is relevant to him. If he is asking about deodorant, talk to him about how he will soon start to smell under the arms like an adult. Go back to the previous chapter and try to work out where your son is, regarding the changes to his body. Talk about the changes that are now happening as well as the ones to come.

Just remember, you don't need to talk to your son about everything. The fact that you are talking to him is much more important than what you say. By talking about puberty, you're actually letting him know that he can turn to you for support, guidance and information.

Feelings

Your son needs to know from the very start that puberty will change his body, but it will also change his feelings as well.

It may help your son to know:

- All these new emotions are normal.

- Feeling anxious about growing up is normal. It is normal to not want to grow up or to even be excited or in a hurry to grow up. It can even be normal to feel as if he is going crazy at times.

- Everyone goes through puberty. Some of his friends will be feeling the same things as him. Or different things.

- Going through puberty can be hard.

- There are ways to express intense feelings. He may need some guidance as to what will work for him, such as going for a run or a swim, writing in a journal, or talking to someone.

- Mood swings may happen, where he might feel sad one moment and happy the next. Life for a few years can sometimes be a rollercoaster of changing emotions.

- He may want to spend more time on his own and alone. He needs to know that is okay and that his parents still love him and are still there for him.

- Privacy will become a lot more important and he needs to know his parents will respect his need for more personal space.

- His brain will be changing and getting ready for him to be an adult. This means that he will want to start making his own decisions about things and to try new things.
- Having sexual feelings is normal and is nothing to feel guilty about. Acting on such feelings, however, is a big responsibility.

Skin care

Your son's skin will now become oily, as his oil glands become more active. The oil glands below the surface of his skin will enlarge and start to make sebum, a white oily substance that keeps the skin moist. Sometimes the sebum gets blocked in the oil glands, which means whiteheads or blackheads appear, and if there is infection, then pimples will appear. This means that he'll have oilier skin, sometimes with acne.

As you start to notice his skin becoming oily, it may help your son to know:

- He needs to wash his face each day.
- He shouldn't pick at or squeeze pimples (risk of infection and scarring).
- Sometimes acne can become severe, and if that happens, you can visit your family doctor for treatment.
- He needs to pull back his foreskin and wash under it. He doesn't need to use soap. Sometimes there is a white substance under the foreskin called smegma. This is normal and healthy, and doesn't need to be washed away, unless the glans is red and inflamed, as it helps to keep the penis healthy.

How much acne will your son have? Chances are that he will have the same amount that you and his other parent had. So, if you didn't have much acne, chances are that your son won't either.

Body odor

Your son will now start to sweat more and develop body odor for the first time. Sweat glands can be found under his arms, on the palms of his hands, at the bottom of his feet and around his groin. During puberty, these sweat glands become more active, and due to the bacteria on his skin, he will start to develop body odor or BO. This means that at times, he'll stink!

As you start to notice his body smelling, it may help your son to know:

- He needs to shower each day.
- He needs to use deodorant or antiperspirant on clean armpits (it doesn't work as well on smelly armpits).
- He will need to wear clean underwear each day.
- He may need to wash his sports shoes or wear cotton/wool/dry-wicking socks if his feet start to smell.
- Everyone sweats, so he isn't alone.

Oily Hair

The oil glands that make your son's skin oilier are the same ones that will now may make his hair oilier. Each strand of hair has its own oil gland, which keeps the hair shiny and waterproof. During puberty, extra oil is produced, which then makes the hair on his head oily. This means that he'll have hair that may look too shiny, oily and greasy.

As you start to notice his hair smelling or looking oily, it may help your son to know:

- He needs to wash his hair more often, possibly daily or every second day.
- He may need to use a special shampoo for oily hair.
- He may need to look for hair styling products that are oil-free or greaseless.

Body and facial hair

As your son goes through puberty, he will start to grow hair in some new places. Pubic hair, meaning hair around the penis and scrotum, usually happens first, with face and chest hair happening much later in puberty. The hair on his arms and legs may also increase and/or change. The amount of hair that your son grows depends on his cultural background and genetics. Some cultures have more hair than others. Have a look at the men on both sides of his family. If they have a lot of body hair, there is a good chance that your son will have a similar amount. Some boys have a lot of hair and some boys don't. Everything is pretty much normal!

Your son will start to grow facial hair between the ages of 14 and 16. Every boy is different, with some boys starting earlier and some later.

As he starts to notice new hair on his body, it may help your son to know:

- He will grow hair at the base of his penis and scrotum. It will start off fine and soft, and over the next couple of years, his pubic hair will grow thicker and darker. It may be coarse or fine, straight or curly. Every boy is different.
- He will start to grow hair under his arms.
- He will grow more hair on his arms and legs, and it may be darker in color.
- He will grow hair on his face, i.e. a beard and a moustache. He may want to remove this by shaving, but you'll talk about it when this hair starts growing.
- The amount of hair that grows is different for everyone.
- Every boy is different. Some boys will have more body hair than others.

Breasts

It is normal for boys (one in two) to have slight chest swelling at the start of puberty due to hormones. It doesn't mean that your son is growing breasts. It is just extra fat tissue that will flatten out in 12-to-18 months' time, when his shoulders grow wider. Boys usually find this quite alarming, as they think that they are growing breasts and that they are there to stay.

If you start to notice breasts, it may help your son to know:

- One in two boys will start to grow breasts.

- This is completely normal and will go away in 12-to-18 months. He won't have breasts forever and he won't need to wear a bra.

- Most boys find this embarrassing.

- If he feels self-conscious, he can try wearing loose fitting shirts, so that it isn't as noticeable.

- Some boys also get tenderness behind the nipple area. This is normal too.

- The skin behind his nipple, the areola, will grow darker and wider.

- Some people will make comments about his changing body. Sometimes these comments are nice or they can be teasing or even mean. Talk to your son about how to manage this. What can he do if this happens to him? Who can he talk to?

- Every boy is different. This will happen to some boys but not all. There is nothing that he can do, other than wait for his shoulders to grow wider, which is when this breast tissue will flatten out.

- His friends are going through the same thing.

Body size and shape

Your son needs to know that he will be having two types of growth spurt. He will grow taller, and he will also start to get heavier as his body builds muscle and stores fat.

As you start to notice his body shape and size changing, it may help your son to know:

- His body will grow taller, heavier and stronger.
- He may feel self-conscious about these changes.
- He may have some growing pains while this happens. The cause is unknown but he may feel it in the legs (calf, front of thigh or behind the knees). It may be worse in the afternoon or evening and may wake him during the night. Massage, heat packs and mild analgesia can help.
- He will gain weight, and this is what his body is supposed to do. His body is going to start building muscle and storing fat, and his bones will grow longer and thicker.
- He may develop stretch marks as his body grows quickly. These will eventually fade over time.
- At times, he may feel fat. This is normal, and when his body has its next growth spurt for height, any extra fat will usually spread out. We all have different body shapes, and a person can't change the body shape he is meant to have.
- He doesn't need to worry about dieting. As long as he has a healthy well-balanced diet and enough exercise, his body will do what it is meant to do.
- There is a wide range of body shapes and sizes.
- His face will change, becoming longer and narrower than it was before.

Voice changes

Your son's voice will change during puberty as his larynx (Adam's apple) increases in size. His vocal chords will become longer and thicker, and the tone of his voice will begin to change. His voice will begin to break or crack, then become low. This usually happens around 14 or 15 but can happen earlier or later. It may happen suddenly, or he may not even notice it.

It may help your son to know that:

- His voice might crack when he speaks. This is when his voice will suddenly shift to a higher pitch, and temporarily sound high and squeaky.

- Some boys find this really embarrassing, while other boys aren't all that bothered.

- Try not to make this a big deal when it happens. The more he worries, the more it will crack.

- It is a sign that he is growing up.

- It is happening to other boys too.

- Girls' voices change too, but not as much as boys.

Penis

Your son needs to know that his penis will be changing too. As well as growing bigger, erections will be much more frequent and he will begin to ejaculate.

It may help your son to know that:

- His penis will grow longer before it grows wider.

- Penises come in all shapes and sizes. Some are long, some are short. Some are wide and some are narrow.

- Bigger penises are not always better. Sex is about more than the size of your penis.

Pearly penile papules

All penises are different, and it is normal for some penises to have pearly penile papules. These are little flesh-colored bumps that form a ring around the base of the glans, the 'head' of the penis. They are all about the same size and shape and they do not bleed, itch, or hurt.

It may help your son to know that:

- Every penis is different.

- Some penises can have pearly penile papules. These are little bumps under the head of the penis.

- They are more common in boys with a foreskin, but can still be found on circumcised penises.

- Sometimes they can be mistaken for warts.

- A man may not know he has them until a sexual partner tells him. Some men don't notice them until they are adults.

- They are perfectly normal and are a healthy variation. They do not need to be removed.

- Most boys (and men) worry when they first find them.

PEARLY PENILE PAPULES

Circumcision

Your son needs to know that some penises look different for a reason. Some boys will have a circumcised penis, where the foreskin, or skin at the end of the penis, is removed.

CIRCUMCISION

BEFORE CIRCUMCISION

AFTER CIRCUMCISION

It may help your son to know that:

- Some boys will have a different-looking penis because they have been circumcised.

- Circumcision is a medical procedure where the foreskin, the skin at the end of the penis, is removed.

- It can happen for cultural or religious reasons. It can also happen for medical reasons, when the foreskin is too tight to be pulled back (retracted).

- Some boys are circumcised when they are infants, children or even adults.

- A circumcised penis still works the same for boys. He will still have erections, and ejaculate.

Testicles

One of the first physical changes that will happen to your son during puberty will be to his testicles. Over the next few years, they will slowly start increasing in size, as they develop the parts necessary to make sperm.

It may help your son to know that:

- His testicles will start to grow bigger and to hang lower.
- They can range in size from big to small. Bigger does not mean better.
- His testicles are very sensitive. In some sports, he may need to wear a box or jock strap to protect them from being damaged.
- Testicles have two jobs to do – to make sperm, and to make androgens (the male hormones).
- The skin on his scrotum will start to change and become thinner, redder, pimply/bumpy.
- His scrotum can shrink when cold, swimming in cold water, and stretch when warm, after a hot bath.
- Testicles like to stay at a constant temperature, around two-to-four degrees cooler than normal body temperature. This is why they move around in the scrotum.
- In late puberty, he needs to start checking his testicles for signs of testicular cancer, such as lumps or bumps. Once a month, he should roll his testicle between his thumb and three fingers when in a hot shower or bath. The testicle should feel soft and smooth like a boiled egg that has been peeled.

Erections

Your son needs to know that he will start having more erections as he goes through puberty. This is a normal part of puberty and it happens to all boys.

It may help your son to know that:

- An erection is when his penis becomes stiff and hard, larger and longer, and stands out from the body.

- He has been having erections since he was a baby, but they will now happen a lot more.

- There are lots of different slang terms for erections, such as 'boner' and 'hard on'.

- His penis can feel hard as if there is a bone inside, but there isn't. There is lots of spongy tissue instead, which gets hard when it is filled with blood.

- Erections can happen slowly or very quickly.

- Some boys worry about the size of their penis. Usually, there is nothing to worry about, and it will be the right size penis for them. Penises shown on porn videos are not normal and are chosen because they are unusually large.

- His penis will always look smaller when he is looking down at it. Tell him to try standing in front of a mirror, and he will see the difference.

- He doesn't have to ejaculate just because his penis is erect.

- Pre-ejaculatory fluid, or pre-cum, is a small amount of clear liquid that comes out of the penis when sexually aroused.

- An erect penis can stick out at different angles, or it may stand nearly straight up. When erect, it may be straight, curve to the right or the left, or some other way. No matter what the angle is, it's perfectly normal.

- Everyone's penis is different.

Unwanted erections

It may help your son to know that erections can happen for lots of different reasons. He might have a full bladder, his clothes might be rubbing against his penis, or he might be having some sexy thoughts. They can also happen for no reason at all. This can be embarrassing for boys, and they need to be reminded that all boys (and men) have unwanted erections. As their hormones settle, they won't happen as often.

Some tips for managing unwanted erections:

- Wear baggy pants and long shirts if they keep on happening.
- Hold school books or a bag in front of an erection.
- Sit down when having an erection.
- Put hands in pockets to try and hide it.
- Tie a jumper/shirt around the waist and let the sleeves cover it.
- Try to focus on something else until it goes away.
- Remember, it is more noticeable to the person having an erection than to anyone else!

Ejaculation

Early in puberty, your son will start to make sperm. It takes a few years until his body is ready for ejaculation. This usually happens when boys are aged 13 to 14, sometimes older, or even younger, and nearly always through masturbation or by having a wet dream.

It may help your son to know that:

- One day, some fluid will come out of the hole at the end of his penis.
- This only happens when his penis is erect. It can happen when masturbating, during sex and during a wet dream.
- He needs to be having sexy thoughts and to be sexually aroused for ejaculation to happen. It won't just happen because he has an erection.
- This is something that happens to all boys (and men) and will happen for the rest of his life.
- This fluid is called semen, and it contains his sperm. Sperm is needed to help make a baby:
  - About one teaspoon of white, creamy semen is ejaculated, sometimes less (1/2 tsp) or more (2 tsp).

- o Semen comes out in five-or-six spurts, sometimes more or less. It is more likely to dribble out in young boys rather than spurt.
- Semen is different from pre-ejaculatory fluid (or pre-cum), which is a small amount of clear liquid that comes out of the penis when sexually aroused.
- Once he starts to ejaculate, he is fertile, which means that he could make a baby and become a father.

Wet dreams

During puberty, boys will start to have wet dreams, or nocturnal emissions. Not all boys have wet dreams, but it is better that your son know that they are normal, than to worry that there is something wrong with his penis.

It may help your son to know that:

- He might experience something called a wet dream.
- A wet dream happens when he is asleep.
- The penis becomes erect and ejaculates while he is sleeping. He might wake up just as he is about to ejaculate, as he is ejaculating, or just after ejaculation.
- He might not wake up at all. This means that he may wake up with a wet patch in his pajama pants or in his bed.
- Sometimes, the semen has dried up before waking, and he may just find a slight watermark.
- Wet dreams are normal and natural.
- He can't stop himself from having wet dreams.
- Not all boys have them; it is normal whether he does or doesn't.
- Some boys find them embarrassing, and that's okay.
- He can start changing his own sheets, or doing his own washing, if he isn't comfortable with anyone knowing about it.

Masturbation

During puberty, your son might discover that touching or rubbing his penis can feel nice. His penis will become erect, he'll ejaculate and experience orgasm. Masturbation is not harmful as long as it is kept private. There is no scientific evidence that it causes any harm to the body or mind. It is only a problem when it stops a person from doing other things, or when it is done in public. However, there are many religious and cultural beliefs around masturbation.

It may help your son to know:

- Masturbation is often the first way boys can experience sexual pleasure.
- Many boys and girls begin to masturbate for sexual pleasure during puberty.
- Some boys and girls never masturbate. This is normal too.
- Ejaculation doesn't always follow masturbation.
- Some boys masturbate more frequently than others.
- Too much masturbation is when it stops him from doing things or if his penis gets sore.
- A body can't run out of sperm. It is always making new sperm.
- If he doesn't masturbate or have wet dreams, the sperm will just be reabsorbed in his body. This isn't harmful.
- Masturbation does not cause physical or mental harm.
- Some cultures and religions oppose masturbation (talk to your religious leader).
- The decision about whether to masturbate is a personal one.
- Masturbation is a private activity.
- Many adults masturbate at some time in their lives.

Sexual feelings

During puberty, your son will experience sexual feelings for the first time in his life. The hormones that are busy making his body fertile are also making sure that he'll want to have sex so he can help to make a baby, which means he will start to have sexual thoughts, and be sexually attracted to either girls or boys.

It may help your son to know:

- During puberty, it is normal to become more aware of the opposite (or same) sex, and to feel more sexual.

- It is also normal to not experience sexual feelings. Asexuality is when someone is uninterested in sex or feels no desire for sex.

- Some boys will experience stronger or weaker sexual feelings than others. Some boys will start to have sexual feelings sooner or later than other boys. Everyone is different.

- In boys, the main physical sign of sexual excitement is an erect penis. In girls, it is wetness of the vagina.

- Another sign of sexual arousal for boys is pre-ejaculatory fluid (or pre-cum), which is a small amount of clear liquid that comes out of the penis. It is made by the Cowper's gland (along the urethra) and provides lubrication and helps to change the pH of the vagina, so that the sperm makes it through the vagina. It may have some sperm in it, which means that technically a girl could become pregnant from pre-ejaculatory fluid.

- Sexual feelings can come from reading a romantic novel, watching a movie, or thinking about another girl or boy.

- Having sexual feelings is normal and is nothing to feel guilty about.

- Acting on such feelings with a partner is a big responsibility, and it is best to wait until older.

Conception

Puberty happens for one reason – reproduction. This is so your son can help to make a baby and start the next generation. He needs to know that this can happen and how it happens.

It may help your son to know:

- A baby is made when an egg from a female joins with sperm from a male.
- This can happen during sexual intercourse, when a man's penis is in a woman's vagina.
- Their bodies move together and after a short time, semen containing sperm comes out of the penis.
- The sperm travels up through the uterus and into the fallopian tubes. If one strong sperm joins with an egg, a baby begins to form.
- Babies can also be made with medical assistance, such as in vitro fertilization (IVF) or surrogacy.

Sex

Talking about puberty means also talking about sex. As puberty progresses, your son is going to start thinking of sex differently. Before puberty, he only thought of sex in a theoretical way, as something adults do. Now, as his hormones rewire him to reproduce, he will start to think of sex as something that he will want to do. This means you need to start talking to your son about sex. If you have never talked about sex with him before, don't expect him to be totally ignorant. It is very possible that he will have heard other kids talk about sex or have read about it.

When talking to your son, it is important to remember that sex is more than the type of sexual activity that makes a baby. It can include oral sex, anal sex, and lots of touching where no penetration happens at all. Sex can also happen in lots of different ways. It might happen between two people who are in a loving and committed relationship, but it can also happen between two people who have only just met. Your son will hear a lot of mixed negative messages about sex and may need some help trying to interpret them.

When talking about sex, there are two parts to the conversation. First, it is about giving your son information or the facts, for example, sex can be when the man puts his penis inside the woman's vagina.

Second, it is about providing him with some guidelines about what is appropriate behavior, for example, you think he should wait until he is married, or in a loving committed relationship, before he has sexual intercourse.

It is important that you tell your son what sexual attitudes and behaviors are okay, and not okay, in your family. And don't just tell him what they are. You need to explain why you feel this way, so your son can understand. Knowing the 'why' will help him while he is forming his own sexual values.

It may help your son to know:

- Sex can be lots of different things, but usually when you hear people talking about it, they mean sexual intercourse.
- Adults have sex for lots of different reasons:
  o To make a baby.
  o It feels good (it can also feel awful).
  o For fun.
  o It is a way to show love or to get close to someone.
- Sex is something that is just for adults. It isn't for kids and it isn't something that you should do with members of your family.
- Sex is something that is private and should only happen when … (share your beliefs about when it is okay for him to think about sex).
- Sex is special and is something that should happen with someone that you trust and care deeply about.

Consent

This is the age where you need to talk about consent in more detail. For the first time, your son is starting to explore what sex means. As you start to talk about sex, you also need to talk about consent for sex. Learning about consent will take many conversations.

It may help your son to know:

- Consent is when you agree to do something, or you allow something to happen to you.
- In some situations, it isn't possible to give consent, such as when under the influence of drugs or alcohol.
- How to give or withhold consent and ask for it from others.
- How to seek help when he, or someone else, is having their right to consent violated.
- The consequences of not respecting consent, such as sexual assault, rape, or sex with a minor.
- Consent can be partial, for example, it is okay to do this but not this. 'You can kiss me, but don't put your hands down my pants'.
- It is okay to change your mind later on, for example, you can withdraw consent at any time.

Same sex attraction

During puberty, your son will discover whether he is attracted to girls or boys. Some boys will already know this, but some won't have given it much thought until now. One in every 10 boys will be attracted to the same sex. It is possible that your son will be same-sex attracted. Who your son is attracted to is not his choice. He can't choose to like girls instead. It just isn't possible. He can try, but it won't work.

By now, he'll have already worked out that most boys like girls. It is what he sees on TV, reads about in books, and sees around him. He will have also heard negative comments being made about gays, and he will have picked up on the fact that it isn't something that society as a whole is supportive about. Which means that for same-sex attracted boys, this can be a confusing time in which he will need your support. Whether you believe that same-sex attraction is okay or not okay, you still need to talk to your son about the fact that some kids are attracted to the same sex, and not the opposite sex. All children need to know that sexual orientation is not a choice, all people deserve respect regardless of their sexual orientation, and who we are attracted to, whether it be girls or boys, is only a small part of who we are.

Just remember to discuss this topic with care and sensitivity, regardless of your beliefs. Sexual attraction is not a choice. If your son ends up being attracted to the same sex, how will he feel about it and will he feel safe talking to you about it?

It may help your son to know:

- Puberty is the time we discover which sex we are attracted to.

- He may feel attracted to the opposite or same sex. He may feel attracted to both sexes, or he may not feel attracted to anyone. This is all normal.

- He will either like girls or boys, both or none. In time, he will know who he likes.

- He cannot change who he is attracted to.

- All people deserve respect regardless of their sexual orientation.

- Who we are attracted to, whether girls or boys, is only a small part of who we are.

- He needs to know about homophobia, and that some religions and cultures believe that same-sex attraction (homosexuality) is wrong.

Preventing pregnancy

Your son won't need a lot of information about contraception until he is showing an interest in girls or boys. You can give him the information, but it won't really be relevant until he is thinking about being sexually active. But he does still need to know that women can choose to prevent pregnancy.

It may help your son to know:

- When a man and a woman want to have sexual intercourse without having a child, they can use a family planning method to prevent pregnancy.

- There are many types of family planning methods, also called contraceptives:
  - o Abstinence, condom, implants, pill, injections, morning after pill.
- A boy cannot become pregnant if they have sex with another boy.
- Unprotected sex means having sexual intercourse without any contraception.
- Some religions and cultures are against the use of contraception.

Sexually transmitted infections (STIs)

Your son won't need a lot of information about STIs until he is showing an interest in girls or boys. You can give him the information but it won't really be relevant until he is thinking about being sexually active. He does still need to know that there are infections that can be spread through sexual contact.

It may help your son to know:

- STIs are spread through sexual contact, which includes sexual intercourse and anal or oral contact. Some examples of STIs are:
  - o Syphilis, gonorrhea, chlamydia, genital herpes, trichomoniasis, hepatitis B, human papilloma virus (HPV), and HIV.
- He can protect himself by using condoms and not having sexual contact with an infected person.
- STIs aren't nice things to have:
  - o The symptoms for men can include painful urination, urethral discharge, ulcers, or sores, depending on the STI.
  - o The symptoms for women include genital sores or ulcers, lower abdominal pain or tenderness, unusual vaginal discharge, vaginal itching, painful urination, or painful sexual intercourse, depending on the STI.

- STIs need to be treated with medication or they can cause serious problems.

- Some STIs cause permanent infertility, chronic pain, and cancer. Without treatment, heart and brain damage can develop 10-to-25 years after initial exposure to syphilis.

- Sex is not free of risks.

Online safety

As your son goes through puberty, he will become more curious about sex. He will also become more independent and not always come to you with his questions. Instead, he will head to the next best thing – the internet – to search for answers. He is going to stumble across sexually-explicit content – in the form of pornography – in his search for knowledge. He will also find information that looks reliable but isn't.

It may help your son to know:

- What your family rules are regarding the safe use of internet-enabled devices, as well as the consequences if he breaks these rules.

- Sometimes it is hard to tell whether information on the internet is reliable or not.

- He will stumble across sexually-explicit images online (if he hasn't already). If he does, he should turn off the device and inform an adult that he trusts. Remind him that he won't get into trouble.

- Porn is not the best way to learn about sex. If he has any questions, he can ask you, or find the answer in an age-appropriate book or website.

- Sending and receiving naked photos of private parts is illegal, until he is legally deemed an adult. The age varies in different countries but it is usually 16.

Girl changes

There are some girl changes that your son should also know about. It may help your son to know:

- Girls can orgasm too, with a partner or when masturbating.
- Girls can have erotic dreams (sometimes you hear them called wet dreams).
- Girls aren't fertile all the time, just for a few days each month.
- Girls menstruate (bleed) or have a period for three-to-five days every month.

How To Talk About Puberty

It isn't what you say that matters. What matters is that you're giving your child the message that you're open to talking to them about anything, no matter what.

Getting started

The hardest part of talking to kids about puberty is getting started. You know what you can talk about, but how do you actually say it? How do you start the conversation?

It is normal to feel a little uncomfortable when you first start talking about puberty with your son. We all do. Many of us didn't have comfortable conversations with our own parents, growing up. We don't have any helpful memories of what to do, just lots of memories of what not to do! Like with all new things, it will get easier. The more often you talk with your son about puberty, the easier it will get.

You'll find many suggestions on different ways to start talking with your son about puberty. Try to pick just one to start with, rather than trying to do them all. Choose one that feels comfortable, or like something you may already be doing. For example, if you already buy books for your son, buying a book on puberty is a great way to start.

Key messages

So, what are the main messages that you need to give your son?

- He isn't alone!
- You've been through puberty too, so you do understand what it may be like for him.
- He can talk to you about anything, no matter what.
- You will answer his questions truthfully.
- If you don't know the answer, you will find it and get back to him with it.
- What sexual attitudes and behaviors are okay, and not okay, in your family.
- He is normal!

At the end of the day, it isn't about how much information you share. It is about the fact that you are talking openly about growing up. This means that you will have an open relationship where your son can talk to you about anything, no matter what. As a parent, that is pretty much what we all want.

Everyday approach

The best approach with talking is to keep it as much like an everyday conversation as possible. If your son can sense a lecture coming on, he will tune out and stop listening almost immediately. Make sure you use an everyday tone and language. Try to talk about sperm in the same voice and way that you would use when talking about his plans for the weekend. By sounding everyday (or natural), you are letting him know what is happening to him is normal and nothing to be ashamed of.

Get ready to repeat yourself, as you will need to have many conversations on the one topic before he will fully understand what you've been saying. This is completely normal and the way his brain works.

Try to tell him a little bit more than you think he needs to know. As parents, we automatically tend to err on the side of caution and tell our kids less than they need to know, especially when it comes to love, sex and relationships.

Don't assume that he is too young or not ready for it. If he isn't ready, he'll just forget whatever it is that you said. When he is ready for that bit of information, he'll probably let you know.

Don't forget to listen, too. Listen to what he has to say, or what he thinks. He probably knows a lot more than you think he does.

When starting late

If you've never talked about any of this stuff before, it isn't too late to start, even if your son already has hair in new places, a deep voice, or is taller than you.

So, what's the best way to get started?

First, you need to warn your son that you are going to start talking about puberty and growing up. You could try explaining that you've realized that you haven't talked about puberty before, but that you would like to change that.

You could try saying:

- *A book I'm reading is about puberty. I know we haven't really talked about puberty before, but I'm going to try to change that, so we can have conversations about it.*

- *A book I'm reading made me realize how important it is for parents to talk with their kids about puberty. Since we haven't talked about it before, I'd like to start.*

Second, explain why you haven't talked to him about puberty and growing up before.

You could try saying:

- *It's something that my parents didn't talk about very much when I was a kid.*

- *I've always been worried that I would be bringing it up at the wrong time or the wrong place.*

- *I've always worried that I would get it all wrong or do as bad a job as my parents did.*

- *I've always been worried about saying too much or too little or even saying the wrong thing.*

- *Talking about sex makes me feel really uncomfortable.*

Third, explain what is going to change.

You could try saying:

- *I want us to be able to talk about anything, including sex. You are going to hear me talking about puberty and growing up. If you have any questions or want to talk about something, I want you to know that I am always available.*

Getting past your fears and worries

A lot of parents wonder if they are doing the right thing.

Maybe your son is too young for all this? Maybe or maybe not. Puberty happens whether kids are emotionally ready for it or not. Isn't it better that your son is prepared for the changes that will soon be happening to him, and for him to know that he can turn to you for support, guidance and information?

Won't you be encouraging him to be sexual? No, not at all. All you're doing is giving him information about what will be happening to him. You're also guiding him, because you're telling him what sexual behavior and attitudes are okay, and not okay, in your family. Research tells us that kids who have received good sex education are less likely to be sexually active and when they are, they will be much safer than their uneducated peers.[4]

He hasn't asked any questions yet, so maybe he isn't interested? Some boys ask questions and some don't. But it doesn't mean that he isn't interested. It just means that you will have to be the first one to bring it up.

Maybe you will say too much, or not enough, or even the wrong thing? Possibly, but it doesn't really matter if you do. What matters is that you are showing your son that you are willing to talk to him

---

4 SRE – the evidence. 2015. Evidence briefing. Sex Education Forum http://www.sexeduca-tionforum.org.uk/evidence.aspx

about puberty, love, sex and relationships. You are letting him know that he can come and talk to you about anything. That's what really matters.

Getting comfortable with talking

It is normal for both parents and kids to feel uncomfortable talking about puberty. Luckily for you, it does get easier the more do it.

There are some things that you can do to help manage embarrassment:

- Let your son know if you sense that he is uncomfortable talking about puberty. Try saying:
  - o *Some kids can feel really uncomfortable talking about puberty with their parents. I totally get it! I feel awkward talking about it too. Maybe we can help each other get past the awkwardness.*

- Let your son know that you feel embarrassed. Try saying something like:
  - o *I feel a bit uncomfortable talking about puberty because my parents never talked with me about it. But this is an important subject, so I really want to talk with you about it.*

- Keep it simple and talk about one topic at a time. Decide what you want to talk about, such as the need to wear deodorant to manage body odor. Spend a moment, and think about the best way to casually bring up the topic. You might say:
  - o *Hey, I bought this for you at the supermarket today* (show him the deodorant). *Now that you're going through puberty, you'll sweat more and stink! This will help you to stink less. You just spray it onto each underarm. Just like this* (apply deodorant to yourself). *Does that make sense?*

- Talk when you're doing something else, such as washing dishes; this makes it seem like an everyday topic and not something to be ashamed of.

- Take a deep breath and take your time to respond to questions. There is no rush!

- Use humor. You don't have to make a joke about it, but laughing about puberty shows that it is a normal topic.

- Get some puberty books to read with your son. This way you don't have to stress about remembering what to say, as all the information is there in the book.

Sharing values

Don't forget to also talk about what sexual attitudes and behaviors are okay, and not okay, in your family. Don't just talk about the fact that you can prevent pregnancies with contraception. Share with your son what your thoughts are about contraception and unplanned pregnancy. Explain the reasons behind your belief so that your son understands why.

Don't just tell your son what sex is all about. Also let him know when you think it is a good time for him to think about sex. It might not be until he is married, or of legal age, or he must be in a loving, committed relationship first. Again, explain why, so that your son can understand the reasoning behind your beliefs.

Try to get into the habit of explaining what you think or believe when talking about love, sex and relationships. This is your opportunity to guide your son as he grows up, and to help him make healthy decisions around love, sex and relationships.

Share stories

Most kids are interested in hearing their parents' stories about growing up. Sharing stories about what puberty was like for you reassures your son that you do know what he is going through. Plus, it is a great way to build connection and trust with your child.

Try saying things like:

- *I remember when I found my first pubic hair. I didn't know I would get hair down there, so I found some scissors and cut it off.*

- *I remember my first kiss. I really liked this person and one weekend at a party, we found a dark corner and kissed. All I really remember is this cold wet tongue being poked into my mouth, lots!*

- *I remember when I first started to like boys. I used to think about them all the time and daydream about being their girlfriend.*

- *I asked your dad what he used to do when he was a boy and had wet dreams. He said that he used to use an old shirt and then throw it into the bottom of the wash basket. It was something that he felt really embarrassed about and it was something that his parents never talked about.*

Take it slow

When talking to kids about puberty, there is no rush. Today, we know that the best way for kids to learn is through lots of frequent, repetitive conversations. If your son looks like he isn't listening, don't despair. He probably is listening, but he's hiding his discomfort by pretending not to. Keep on talking regardless. Just make sure you keep it conversational, don't turn it into a lecture and don't overdo it. Maybe keep it to one or two comments a week.

By keeping the conversation open, you are letting him know that he can come and talk to you about anything.

Be available

By talking to your son about puberty and growing up, you are letting him know that you are available and willing to talk. Make sure you tell him that he can come to you with any questions or concerns at any time. Don't be too pushy or obvious. You've got plenty of time to talk about all this stuff – there is no rush. If he throws you an opportunity to talk, make sure you grab it and talk. Yes, life does get busy, but five or 10 minutes of your time is often all that he needs.

Try to encourage him to talk about how he feels about growing up and changing. Ask him what he's looking forward to and what he's nervous about.

Normalize it

It is really important to normalize puberty for your son. He needs to know that what is happening to him is completely normal, and it is happening to his friends too.

It may help your son to know:

- Everyone is different.
- Some boys start early, some start late.
- Some boys develop fast, some develop slowly.
- Sometimes it can feel out of control.
- Going through puberty can be hard:
  - o Your emotions swing.
  - o Your body changes.
  - o You start to have sexual feelings.
  - o Your relationships with family and friends begins to change.
- His body is doing what it is meant to do.

Indirect questions

Listen for indirect questions or disguised questions from your son. Some kids can be a bit vague and it may not be very clear what they are really asking about. Make sure you check back with your son and confirm that you have understood his question, and that you've given him enough information.

You could try saying:

- *Did that answer your question?*
- *Does that make sense?*
- *Was there anything else you wanted to know?*
- *Do you have any more questions?*

Find out what they already know

Kids can ask some very interesting questions. Sometimes though, there can be more than one answer, like the question, 'Where do I come from?'. There are many answers to this question – from hospital, my uterus, out of my vagina, from the apes. A good trick for working out what it is that your son is asking, is to ask him what he thinks. Instead of answering your question straight away, try asking him, 'What do you think?'. This way, you can also work out what he already knows and just fill in the gaps.

Kids often dwell on a topic before they ask their questions, so he probably already knows the answer but just wants confirmation.

When you don't know the answer

Your son will ask you questions to which you don't know the answer. No one knows everything and I can guarantee that he is already asking you questions you don't have the answer for. The best way to manage this is to be completely honest and say, 'I don't know'. Then tell him that you'll find out and get back to him with an answer. If the topic isn't too risqué, you could both go and google it, or look it up in a book together. Just be careful when googling topics about puberty and sex, as you will often find pornography or content that isn't age-appropriate. Whatever you do, don't forget to get back to him with the answer. Forgetting could signal to your son that you aren't reliable, that the topic is taboo, or that you aren't comfortable answering these types of questions. This means that he'll start to look elsewhere for answers, which isn't a good thing.

Delaying answers

Sometimes, we just can't answer questions straight away. Your son may have asked you a question at the wrong time or the wrong place, or maybe you are just too busy or too uncomfortable to answer it on the spot. It is helpful if you can have your standard response to untimely questions worked out in advance. Acknowledge that he asked a question and explain when you'll respond.

You could try saying:

- *That's a great question, but how about we talk about that when we get home?*

- *I'm not sure about that. How about we talk about that later when I'm not so busy?*

- *You know what, I don't know. How about I find out the answer and I get back to you with it?*

If you get forgetful, send yourself an email, or post a note somewhere to remember. When you find the answer, you can restart the conversation with something as simple as, 'Remember how you asked me about erections earlier today? Well, I found the answer to your question'.

Third person

Talking in the third person can sometimes make it a bit less uncomfortable, for both you and your son.

You could try saying:

- *I saw your friend Tom the other day, and noticed that he's gotten really tall. It made me think that maybe we should be starting to talk about puberty and the changes that your body will be going through.*

- *One of the moms was talking today about how her daughter has started her period. It made me realize that we haven't really talked about the changes that happen to girls as they go through puberty.*

- *I heard a story on the radio today, where an expert was talking about how many boys don't understand what puberty is. Have any of your friends talked about puberty yet, or about any of the changes that are happening to them?*

Books

Books make talking about puberty a lot easier. There are a lot of puberty books that have been written specifically for boys. They'll provide your son with all the information he needs to know. You don't have to worry about trying to remember everything. Plus, the information in books is usually accurate, reliable, and written age-appropriately in language that our sons will understand.

Some books are written for younger boys and will only talk about puberty and the changes that will happen. These books don't talk about sex, mainly because they target a younger audience, such as eight-to-11-year-old boys. There are also books that talk about puberty and growing up. Growing up always includes topics like love, sex, relationships, contraception, etc. These topics are always talked about in an age-appropriate way and are what 12-to-14-year-old boys are curious about.

Choosing the right book comes down to a number of things, such as the age of your son, his level of reading and how much information you are happy letting him have. If he is young, you'll want a book that won't overwhelm with too much detailed information, or talk about sex. You can get him a more detailed book later on.

Your instinct may be to go with a book that doesn't talk about love, sex and relationships. If he is really young (eight-10), or quite immature compared to his peers, that's fine. But do remember that you aren't protecting him by withholding information. If anything, you are leaving your son vulnerable, as he will just turn to his peers or the internet instead.

You can read the book together, or your son can have it to read alone. If he is reading it alone, just make sure that he knows that he can come to you with any questions.

You could try saying:

- *I heard about this great book on puberty so I bought a copy of it. We can read it together if you like.*

- *You've now reached an age where your body is going to start changing from being a kid to a grownup. I've bought a book that we can read together that talks about what will happen and why. How about we start reading it together tonight?*

- *Joe's mom told me about a book on puberty that she bought Joe to read. I bought you a copy to read by yourself, if you like. If you want to talk about anything in it with me, that would be great.*

To talk about the book later, you could try saying:

- *Remember how we read that book about puberty, well, I was wondering if you had any questions?*
- *I heard something on the radio today about wet dreams. Does that puberty book that I bought you talk about wet dreams?*

To choose a puberty book you can visit your local library or bookshop. You will find a lot of puberty books listed and reviewed in this book review site: Sex Education Books for Children. (http://sexedrescue.com/sex-education-books-for-children/)

Answering personal questions

Your son may ask you some personal questions about puberty and sex that you won't feel comfortable answering. He might ask you about your first period, or about the first time you had sex. If the question is too personal, you don't need to answer it. See it as an opportunity to reinforce privacy but also try to turn it into an educational opportunity.

You could try saying:

- *That is a personal question that I'm not comfortable answering. But I know that it is illegal for children to have sex until they are 16.*
- *Some stuff is private and personal, so I don't really want to answer that question. But I know that they talk about that in your puberty book, so let's go and see what it has to say about it.*

Teachable moments

An easy way to provide information to your son is to find an everyday situation and turn it into an opportunity to teach something. At first you might find them a little bit hard to find. So, try thinking of one topic, for example, pornography, and start looking for opportunities to chat about porn. It could be a story on the radio, an article in the newspaper, a post that you found on Facebook, a blogpost, or something you read in a book. Once you start looking, you will find opportunities for talking, and teachable moments, everywhere.

Some opportunities for teachable moments could include:

- *Did you hear that story on the news about those teenage boys sharing videos of a drunk girl being raped? They are probably going to end up with a prison sentence for it. What do you think you would do if you were at a party and you saw your friends doing something like that? What could you do?*

- *See those two girls over there on the bench? The ones holding hands and kissing? How hard do you think it was for them to tell their family and friends that they were gay?*

- *Look at this magazine ad? Do you think that all women have bodies like that?*

- *Wow, did you hear the words to that song? It was about oral sex. They say that oral sex is something that teens often do with their first kiss? What do you think of that?*

- (Referring to a TV show or movie that you're both watching together) *Do you think that is right for that girl to have sex with her boyfriend because he says he will leave her if she doesn't?*

- *Can you put these tampons away for me in my bathroom? Did you know that a part of puberty for girls is that they get their period? Do you know why this happens?*

- *Did you see what the ad on TV was about? It was talking about deodorant. You're going to need to start using deodorant sometime soon. A part of growing up is that you'll start to get smelly under the arms.*

Pre-warn them

If you want to talk about a particular topic, for example, wet dreams, let your son know in advance. It pre-warns him and can sometimes make him more receptive to talking.

You could try saying:

- *I want to talk to you this weekend about shaving. It will be just you and me, with no other kids.*

- *I bought a puberty book for you today. I thought we could start reading it together before you go to bed tonight.*

- *Hey, I want to talk to you tonight about a sex/puberty thing. Don't worry, you're not in trouble or anything. I just want to talk.*

Conclusion

Congratulations! The fact that you have bought (and hopefully read) this book, means that your son is a fortunate boy! He is fortunate because he has a parent who:

- Wants to support him as he goes through a major phase of change in his life.

- Is someone he can turn to for the support, guidance and information that he needs, instead of turning to his friends or the internet.

- Wants to make sure that he has a better experience of puberty, than the one they had.

- Wants to talk openly with him about love, sex and relationships, even though sometimes it would be a lot easier to just avoid the topic.

- Is prepared to guide him as he works out what sexual behaviors and attitudes are okay and not okay, instead of leaving him to work it out on his own.

- Is now well prepared to start talking to him about puberty and sex, after reading this book.

So, keep this book as a resource that you can turn to when you need it. *Boy Puberty* will let you know the why, what, when and how of talking to your son about puberty.

And remember, it isn't so much *what* you say that matters, it is that you're talking to your son about growing up, and by talking, your relationship with him will grow stronger as he blossoms into a beautiful young man.

Enjoy the journey!

cath hak

Resources

Resources on puberty can be found at Sex Ed Rescue - https://sexedrescue.com/resources/puberty/

Books for your son can be found at the Sex Ed Rescue book review page, which is always being updated with new books - http://sexedrescue.com/sex-education-books-for-children/

If you have questions to ask or want to connect with other parents on the same journey, you can join my free parent Facebook group: https://www.facebook.com/groups/thatparentgroup/

About the Author

Cath Hakanson has been talking to clients about sex for the past 25 years as a nurse, midwife, sex therapist, researcher, blogger and educator. She's spent the past 10 years trying to unravel why parents (herself included) struggle with sex education. Her solution was to create Sex Ed Rescue, an online resource that simplifies sex education and helps parent to empower their children with the right information about sex, so kids can talk to their parents about anything, no matter what.

Cath has lived all over Australia but currently lives in Perth with her partner, 2 children, and ever-growing menagerie of pets. Despite having an unusual profession, she bakes, sews, and knits for sanity, collects sexual trivia, and tries really hard not to embarrass her children in public. Well, most of the time anyway!

CPSIA information can be obtained
at www.ICGtesting.com
Printed in the USA
LVOW10s2056070218

565713LV00025B/286/P